THE *New York* COLONY

SPIRIT
of America®

THE *New York* COLONY

By Barbara A. Somervill

Content Adviser: Eric Gilg, Department of History, University of
Massachusetts, Amherst, Massachusetts

The Child's World®
Chanhassen, Minnesota

8

THE *New York* COLONY

Published in the United States of America by The Child's World®
PO Box 326 • Chanhassen, MN 55317-0326 • 800-599-READ • www.childsworld.com

Acknowledgments
The Child's World®: Mary Berendes, Publishing Director

Editorial Directions, Inc.: E. Russell Primm, Editorial Director; Melissa McDaniel, Line Editor; Elizabeth K. Martin, Assistant Editor; Olivia Nellums, Editorial Assistant; Susan Hindman, Copy Editor; Joanne Mattern, Proofreader; Kevin Cunningham, Peter Garnham, Ruthanne Swiatkowski, Fact Checkers; Tim Griffin/IndexServ, Indexer; Cian Loughlin O'Day, Photo Researcher; Linda S. Koutris, Photo Selector

Photo
Cover: North Wind Picture Archives; Bettmann/Corbis: 6, 8, 15, 18, 20, 21, 23; Corbis: 24 (David Muench), 29 (Lee Snider; Lee Snider); Getty Images/Hulton Archive: 10, 13, 17, 22, 25, 27, 28, 30, 31, 32, 35; North Wind Picture Archives: 14, 16, 19, 26; Stock Montage: 9, 12, 34.

Library of Congress Cataloging-in-Publication Data
Somervill, Barbara A.
  The New York Colony / by Barbara Somervill.
    p. cm.
"Spirit of America."
Summary: Traces the history of New York State from the hunting of woolly mammoths 11,000 years ago to the explorations of Hudson, Verrazano, and Champlain, to its ratification as the eleventh state in 1788. Includes bibliographical references and index.
  ISBN 1-56766-654-X (lib. bdg. : alk. paper)
 1. New York (State)—History—Colonial period, ca. 1600–1775—Juvenile literature. 2. New York (State)—History—1775–1865—Juvenile
literature. [1. New York (State)—History—Colonial period, ca. 1600–1775. 2. New York (State)—History—1775–1865.] I. Title.
 F122 .S76 2003
 974.7'02—dc21   2002151354

18 27 34

Contents

Chapter ONE

The First New Yorkers

Over time, Native American groups built villages and began to farm in addition to hunting and gathering for food. Each member of the group had a task to do.

LONG AGO, GIANT ELEPHANT-LIKE CREATURES called woolly mammoths and mastodons roamed the land we know today as New York. People arrived in the area about 11,000 years ago to hunt these huge animals. These people also collected berries, roots, and nuts for food. Such people are called hunter-gatherers. They moved often to find food.

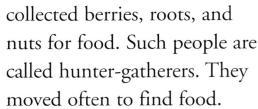

Through many thousands of years, the hunter-gatherers began building villages. People started farming to add to their food supply. The main crops were squash, beans, and corn. As the villages grew, the people formed communities.

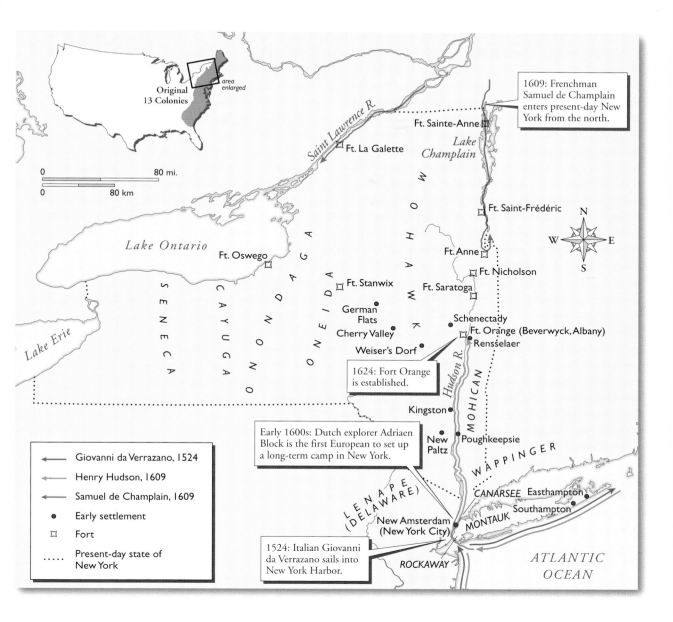

New York Colony at the time of the first European settlement

Several major groups, including the Lenape, the Wappinger, and the Mohican, lived beside the river we call the Hudson. These people hunted deer, beaver, raccoon, bear, and wild turkey. They fished in local streams and harvested crops each fall.

Wampum—beads strung together in a pattern—was the type of money used by Native Americans before the Europeans arrived.

These people all spoke similar languages from the Algonquian language family. This allowed them to speak and trade with each other. They carried trading goods in baskets and clay pots. They used a type of money called wampum. Wampum are beads strung together in a pattern.

By A.D. 900, different Native American peoples moved into central New York. These were the five Iroquois groups: the Seneca, Cayuga, Onondaga, Oneida, and Mohawk.

The Iroquois were called the Haudeno-saunee—the "people of the longhouse." A longhouse was a building that served as home, community center, school, and storehouse.

To build a longhouse, the Iroquois made a wooden frame that they covered with elm bark. A central fire provided heat and a place to cook. Smoke from the fire escaped through a hole in the roof.

Several families lived together in the long-house, which was about 200 feet (60 meters) long. The people living there were related through the women. So, a grandmother and

The Iroquois lived in long-houses. These buildings served as homes several families who were related through the women.

grandfather, her sister and husband, and the grandmother's daughters and their families might live together in a longhouse.

Sometime between 1459 and 1570, the five Iroquois groups formed the **League** of Five Nations. Some people compared the league to a longhouse that stretched 250 miles (400 kilometers) across central New York. The Mohawk guarded the eastern door. The Seneca protected the western entrance. The Oneida and Cayuga formed two squares in the middle. The Onondaga served as keepers of the central fire.

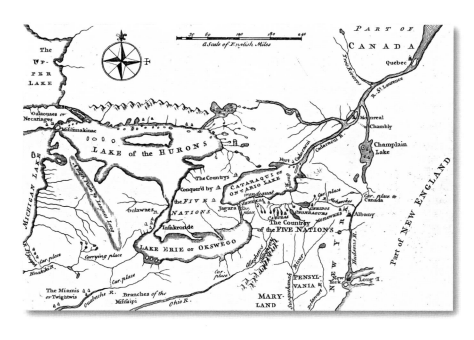

A map created in about 1650 shows the extent of the League of Five Nations.

IROQUOIS LEGEND TELLS OF DEGANAWIDA, THE PEACE MAKER. DEGANAWIDA came from the Huron people, another Iroquois group that lived to the west. Deganawida had a mission. He would bring peace to the Iroquois people under the Great Law. Deganawida explained this to Hiawatha, a Mohawk chief. Hiawatha agreed to follow the Great Law. The two warriors traveled to each Iroquois community to convince other chiefs to agree.

Once they had all agreed to follow the Great Law, Deganawida planted a white pine tree. The pine symbolized peace among the Iroquois. It is said that warriors buried their weapons under the great pine to show they would not war against each other. The phrase "to bury the hatchet" comes from this event. Legend claims that the Peace Maker said:

"The Tree of Peace has four white roots extending to Earth's four corners. . . . If any man or nation shows a desire to obey the Law of the Great Peace, they may trace the roots to their source, and be welcomed to take shelter beneath the Tree."

Chapter TWO

Verrazano, Hudson, and Champlain

Henry Hudson explored the river that now bears his name. He was an Englishman, but sailed for the Dutch East India Company and claimed the land he explored for the Dutch.

IN 1524, GIOVANNI DA VERRAZANO BECAME the first European to see what is now New York when he sailed his ship into New York Bay. Verrazano was an Italian who sailed for the French. There is no record that he ever went ashore or that he claimed land for France.

Eighty-five years later, in 1609, Henry Hudson sailed the same waters as Verrazano had. Hudson was English, but he sailed for the Dutch East India Company. He was searching for a water route to Asia. Hudson sailed his ship, called the *Half Moon,* up the river that now bears his name. He hoped the river led to the Pacific Ocean. He did not realize that the Pacific was 3,000 miles (4,800 km) away! Hudson's search for a sea route to China failed. But his explorations allowed the Dutch to claim land in present-day New York, New Jersey, Delaware, and Connecticut.

Samuel de Champlain founded Quebec as a trading post for the French. He traveled to the area that became New York looking for Native Americans interested in trading furs.

Also in 1609, France's Samuel de Champlain entered New York from the north and headed south. Champlain had already claimed land in present-day Canada for France. He had founded the city of Quebec as a fur trading post. On his trip into New York, Champlain hoped to find Native Americans interested in trading furs. Lake Champlain, between New York and Vermont, is named for this French explorer.

The first European to set up a long-term camp in New York was Dutch explorer Adriaen Block. In 1613, Block's ship burned while anchored off Man-a-hat-ta. We now

Interesting Fact

▶ Because of its importance in the history of American freedom, Lake Champlain is known as the birthplace of the U.S. Navy.

know this place as Manhattan Island. Block's crew was stranded. They lived with local Native Americans for months while building a new ship to take them home. The ship they built could not have survived an ocean trip. Luckily, while at sea, Block's crew met a larger ship that took them home to Holland. Today, people remember Block because an island in Long Island Sound between New York and Rhode Island bears his name.

Areas along the Hudson River were settled by the Dutch East India Company as early as 1614. The settlers came from many nations, including Holland and France. The company assigned farms to the settlers. It also built a number of trading posts, including Fort Orange, which was later renamed Beverwyck and is now the city of Albany.

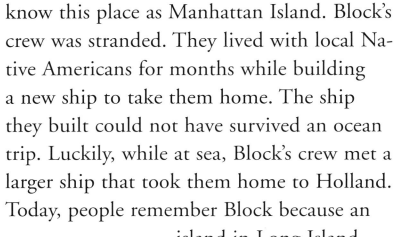

Captain Adrien Block was stranded in North America during his travels and was forced to build a ship for his return voyage.

EXPLORERS HAD IT ROUGH. ENGLISH MERCHANTS HAD HIRED HENRY HUDSON to find a water route to China. After two failed trips, no one in England would hire him again.

In 1609, Hudson convinced the Dutch East India Company to pay for a third voyage. He was to find a water route to China by sailing along the northern coast of Russia. Hudson and his English and Dutch crew sailed from Amsterdam, Holland, on April 6, 1609.

The ship was clumsy and sat too high in the water. It was not good for ocean travel. The crew faced icebergs, high winds, drenching storms, and fog. They threatened to rebel. Hudson agreed to head for North America instead. But they only ran into more violent storms.

Finally, the *Half Moon* reached North America and the mouth of the Hudson River. Hudson traveled up the river later named for him. The water was calmer, but the trip was not. At every stop, the crew met Native Americans. They assumed that the native people planned to rob and kill them. So, the crew kidnapped, killed, and stole from the Native Americans. Hudson didn't accomplish what he had set out to do. But his exploration allowed the Dutch to claim land in North America.

Chapter THREE

The Knickerbockers and the English

Dutch colonists arrive on Staten Island.

THE DUTCH WEST INDIA COMPANY WAS granted a **charter** to settle in North America in 1621 after the Dutch East India Company's charter ran out. The colony was called New Netherland. A 1629 law tried to encourage people to settle the colony. Anyone who arranged for 50 people to settle in New Netherland was given land.

Often those 50 new settlers were **indentured servants.** They worked for landowners to pay off the cost of their trip to New Netherland. Indentured servants had to work for five to seven years to repay their debt.

Dutch settlers in towns were often called knickerbockers because

16

they wore "knickered" pants that ended at their knees. They wore also three-cornered hats and buckled shoes. Knickerbockers lived in such places as New Amsterdam (now New York City), Breukelen (Brooklyn), Schenectady, and Kinderhook.

The Dutch West India Company owned the colony. The company appointed a governor to run New Netherland. The third governor, Peter Minuit, thought himself quite clever when he bought Manhattan Island for $24 worth of beads and trinkets in 1626. He did not realize that the Lenape people he had bought it from did not live on or own the land. Native people

Peter Minuit purchased Manhattan from the Lenape in 1624. He paid them about $24 in beads and trinkets, but did not realize that the Lenape did not live on the island or own the land.

did not believe anyone owned land. Therefore, no one could buy it or sell it.

By 1640, New Amsterdam was a bustling port with 500 people. Unlike the colonies in New England, which were based on religion, the New Amsterdam colony was based on economic **opportunity.** Because of this, it was quite open to people of different religions. The city filled with churches, homes, taverns, and farms. Yes, there were farms on Manhattan!

Families worked their farms together. Crops on Manhattan Island included corn and tobacco. Farther up the Hudson River, farmers grew corn, potatoes, and other vegetables. Orchards produced apples, which were eaten or turned into cider.

Women worked on the farms, helping with planting and harvesting. They also ran the household. They raised and butchered pigs and chickens. They baked bread, cooked meals, and brewed cider and ale. Clothes were made by hand.

Many mothers taught their children at home during colonial times because formal schooling was not readily available.

Towns supported a variety of businesses, including taverns, inns, breweries, and bakeries. There were also tailors, bankers, and shippers. As with farming, men and women worked family businesses together.

Education was not readily available early on in the colony. Children who learned to read, write, and do math usually learned at the kitchen table. Mothers were the colony's first teachers.

In 1638, William Kieft became governor of New Amsterdam. Kieft tried to tax the Native Americans to help him pay for protecting the Dutch settlements. Attacks between the Dutch and the Native Americans became common.

Five years after arriving in New Netherland, Kieft started a small war with the Native Ameri-

William Kieft, shown here addressing a group of colonists, became governor of New Amsterdam in 1638.

Interesting Fact

▶ After being replaced as governor, William Kieft was lost at sea on his way back to Holland.

▸ The business of trading stocks and other properties on Wall Street got a big push in 1792. Early in that year, 24 of New York's leading businessmen met secretly to figure out a way to take complete control of such trading. They signed a treaty called the Buttonwood Agreement, named after the Buttonwood Tree where they usually met. From these roots came today's powerful New York Stock Exchange.

cans. He sent soldiers to kill everyone in a Native American camp in what is now New Jersey. Soon, the Native Americans were in a full-scale war with the Dutch. Kieft asked the Dutch to send more soldiers. Instead, they replaced Kieft with a new governor in 1647. His name was Peter Stuyvesant.

Stuyvesant restored order in the colony. He had a tough manner and a nasty temper. For the most part, the people of New Amsterdam disliked him. But Stuyvesant made a lasting

Wall Street is named after this wooden wall that was built on New York's waterfront to protect the city from attack by Native Americans.

mark on the city. He ordered that city streets be paved with cobblestones. A wall was built at the northern edge of the city to protect the people from attacks by Native Americans. Today, the site of this wall is called Wall Street. It is the heart of the financial district of New York City.

The area we now know as Long Island was then divided between Dutch settlers in the west and English settlers in the east. England's King Charles II did not recognize the Dutch rights to land in North America. He offered his brother, the Duke of York and Albany, a gift. The duke could have New Netherland if he got rid of the Dutch. In 1664, the duke's ships sailed into New Amsterdam. They did not fire a single cannon. New Amsterdam's people gave up the city in the face of England's threat.

The English renamed the colony New York, and Beverwyck became Albany.

Peter Stuyvesant, Dutch governor of New Amsterdam, surrenders the colony to the English without a fight.

THE New-York Weekly JOURNAL.

Containing the freshest Advices, Foreign, and Domestick.

MUNDAY October 14th, 1734.

Mr. *Zenger*;

I Have been Reading, the arguments of Mr. *Smith*, and *Murray*, with Regard to the Courts, and there is one Thing, I can't comprehend, *viz.* If it is the same Court, I take it, that all the Writs ought to be, taken out in *England*, and tested by the Judges there; if they are taken out here, the same Judges ought to test them here. If it is a like Court, it is not the same; and if not the same, it is not that fundamental Court which is established by immemorial Custom. I would be glad some of your Correspondents would clear up this Point; because in my poor Opinion, if the Exchequer Court here is not the same identical Court as the Exchequer Court in *England*, it is without Lawful Authority.

FOREIGN AFFAIRS.

Dantzick, August 4.

Yesterday the Bishop of Cracow, in the King's Name, received Homage of this City, and the Ceremony was very magnificent. His Majesty, before his Departure, issued the Universalia for holding of Petty-Dyets in the Provinces. Those in Polish Prussia, will be held in 15 Days. The Russian and Saxon Troops will march suddenly to the Places where the Provincial Assemblies are to be opened; and the rest are to go and post themselves in Great Poland. M. Rewuski, the Crown Carver, is declared Regimentary, and is to command a Body of Troops, consisting of 2000 Russian Dragoons, 11000 Cossacks, and the Regiment Guards formerly in the Service of King Stanislaus.

Brussels, August 6.

Letters from Rome of the 17th past advise. That they had Advice there that the Siege of Gaeta was not yet formed, altho' the Spaniards had there 70 Cannon, and Mortars, and were working on Batteries, but that all they raised in the Night was beat down next Morning by the Cannon of the Palace; and that the Heats being already Excessive, the Spaniards were in Fear of loosing a vast Number of Men in the Reduction of that Fortress.

Hamburg, August 10.

According to Letters from the Camp before Dantzick, the Vessels there were taken up by Order of the Generals in Chief, to serve for carrying the heavy Artillery and Baggage by Water to Thorn and Warsaw.

We have certain Advice, that King, Stanislaus was departed from Brandenburg Prussia, and arrived safe in the Crown Army, under the Command of M. Kiowski, near Peterkow the 24th past, and immediately afterwards held a Council of War, wherein it was resolved to draw all the dispersed Troops into a Body, and march directly to Volhinia in Podolia.

Amst.

The land across the Hudson became the New Jersey colony.

Between 1670 and 1690, New York's population grew from 5,800 to nearly 14,000 people. Under English rule, New York City grew into one of the most important ports in North America.

Although the English now claimed the New York colony as their own, the Dutch influence remained in some areas. In parts of upstate New York, families continued to speak Dutch. A future president of the United States, Martin Van Buren, would be born in one of these communities in 1783.

In 1735, a trial was held in New York City testing the idea of freedom of the press. John Peter Zenger published a newspaper called the *New York Weekly Journal.* He had attacked the English governor of New York in several articles.

Zenger was arrested and spent a year in jail waiting for his trial. His lawyer said because Zenger had told the truth, he had not committed a crime. The jury found Zenger "not guilty." This case established the idea that newspapers and magazines are free to print the truth in America.

People of many different backgrounds lived in New York. The Dutch had first brought enslaved Africans to New Amsterdam in 1626. (New York would later be the last northern state to outlaw slavery, in 1827.) Sometimes there were tensions between the different groups living in New York City. In 1741, a series of fires raised fears among some whites that enslaved African-Americans were trying to overthrow powerful whites. Thirty blacks and four whites were put to death for taking part in what would be known as The New York **Conspiracy,** or The Great Negro Plot. There is little evidence, however, that there was any organized plot.

The Dutch introduced slavery to the English colonies when they brought a cargo of enslaved Africans to Jamestown in 1619. They brought enslaved Africans to New Amsterdam in 1626.

By 1754, English settlers were eager to move west. Fur trading and farmland in the Ohio River valley could make settlers rich. Both France and Great Britain claimed the region. Competition over this land led Great Britain and France to fight the French and Indian War between 1754 and 1763. The Iroquois, who lived between the British colonies and French Canada, sided with the British. Most of the other Native American groups in New York sided with the French.

Several major battles took place in New York. They included battles at Fort Niagara, Oswego, Fort William Henry, and Fort Ticonderoga. The French won most battles in New York, but they lost the war. In 1763, France agreed to give up all land east of the Mississippi River to Great Britain.

Fort Ticonderoga in New York was built by the French. During the French and Indian War, it was held at various times by the French, English, and American forces.

PETER STUYVESANT (1610?–1672) BEGAN working for the Dutch West India Company in 1635. He worked as a clerk in Brazil. Eight years later, he became governor of Curaçao and several other Caribbean islands. During that time, the Portuguese attacked a Dutch-held island. Stuyvesant lost his leg while fighting the Portuguese. From then on, he wore a wooden leg.

As governor of New Netherland, Stuyvesant achieved mixed results. He improved relations with Native Americans and ran a law-abiding city. But he wielded his power like a club. People called him Old Silvernails or Stubborn Pete.

People did what Stuyvesant wanted or he made them pay. One person threatened to complain to the Dutch West India Company in Amsterdam. Stuyvesant said, "I will make him a foot shorter and send the pieces to Holland, and let him appeal in that way."

When the English came to take over New Netherland in 1664, Stuyvesant wanted to fight. But few people were willing to stand beside the unpopular governor. Stuyvesant was forced to give up, and New Netherland came under English rule.

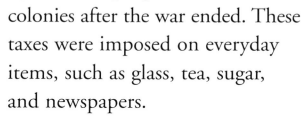

Chapter FOUR

Washington Lost Here

Protecting their interests in North America during the French and Indian War was very expensive for the British government. They wanted colonists to pay taxes to cover the cost of the war.

THE FRENCH AND INDIAN WAR HAD BEEN expensive. The British had to pay for soldiers, supplies, clothing, and food. The British government wanted colonists to pay taxes to cover the costs of the war. They also expected colonists to pay for keeping soldiers in the colonies after the war ended. These taxes were imposed on everyday items, such as glass, tea, sugar, and newspapers.

The taxes angered the colonists. Fifty-six representatives from the colonies met in Philadelphia, Pennsylvania, in 1774, to hold the First **Continental Congress.** The representatives sent a list of their complaints to King George III of Great

Britain. The king ignored the colonists. The colonists were ready to fight for their rights.

In April 1775, brief battles between British soldiers and Massachusetts colonists at Lexington and Concord began the American Revolution. Only weeks later, colonists led by Ethan Allen took over Fort Ticonderoga in northern New York. Allen and his men entered the fort at dawn while the British slept. They captured the fort and weapons needed by the colonists.

Ethan Allen led the colonists who captured Fort Ticonderoga from the British. The attack took the British by surprise.

The Second Continental Congress met in May 1775. The delegates asked George Washington of Virginia to lead the newly formed Continental army. Washington and his men headed to Massachusetts to fight the British.

In March 1776, the British army abandoned Boston. George Washington believed the British would attack New York next because of its important location. If Great Britain controlled New York, the colonies would be cut

Benjamin Franklin, Thomas Jefferson, John Adams, Robert Livington, and Roger Sherman work on the Declaration of Independence.

into two parts. It would be harder to move troops and supplies from one region to another. Washington moved his troops to Manhattan to protect New York.

In the spring, British general William Howe and his ships arrived in New York Bay. Howe had 32,000 men and 30 warships. Washington had only 19,000 men and no navy. He decided to divide his army into small divisions to protect Manhattan, Long Island, and Fort Washington, on the northern tip of Manhattan Island.

That June, Congress asked Thomas Jefferson, Benjamin Franklin, Roger Sherman, and New York's Robert Livingston to write a Declaration of Independence. After a few changes, the document was approved on July 4, 1776. The colonies had cut ties with Great Britain and formed their own country. Washington was preparing to fight the British when he heard the news.

Washington's plan for protecting New York was a disaster. Howe's army poured over Long

Island and headed west into Brooklyn. Washington's troops were poorly trained. The larger, professional British army frightened many of Washington's soldiers. His troops often broke their lines and ran away.

The Continental army met the British in the Battle of Harlem Heights on September 16. Harlem Heights was one of the few New York battles that Washington won.

Two months later, the Continental army tried to hold Fort Washington. It was the last land they held on Manhattan Island. Eight thousand British soldiers attacked the fort.

The Morris-Jumel Mansion served as General George Washington's headquarters during the Battle of Harlem Heights in 1776.

Among the American troops was Margaret Corbin, wife of soldier John Corbin. When British fire killed her husband, Margaret Corbin took over firing his cannon. She was one of the first women to actually fight in an American Revolution battle.

The early New York campaign was a failure. Washington lost New York to the British. The Continental army moved south to New Jersey.

About one-third of the battles in the American Revolution were fought in New York. In most of these battles, the colonists were defeated. Even Fort Ticonderoga was given up to the British without a fight in July 1777.

The colonies' first great victory came in 1777 at the Battle of Saratoga in upstate New York. This was the turning point in the war. With help from the French, the Continental army was able to defeat the British.

The American Revolution finally ended in 1783. The colonists had won their independence from Britain.

British General John Burgoyne surrenders at the Battle of Saratoga.

COLONISTS DID NOT LIKE THE TAXES THAT THE BRITISH WERE IMPOSING ON THEM. They said they were being taxed without having any say in British government.

The first of these taxes was the Sugar Act of 1764. This law made such items as cloth, coffee, wine, and sugar more expensive for colonists. A year later, the British passed the Stamp Act, which taxed all printed materials. The colonists had to pay taxes on wills, newspapers, dice, and playing cards. The Quartering Act soon followed. This law required the colonies to feed and house British soldiers at their own expense. In many cases, soldiers lived in the colonists' homes and ate their food. The Townshend Acts of 1767 added taxes to glass, lead, paint, paper, and tea. The Townshend Acts were the last straw for colonists.

In Boston, a group of men emptied a ship's cargo of tea into Boston Harbor. This act became known as the Boston Tea Party. A second "tea party" was held in Baltimore Harbor. Across the colonies, citizens protested what they called taxation without **representation.**

Chapter FIVE

The Eleventh State

George Clinton served as the first governor of the state of New York. He went on to serve as vice president of the United States from 1805 to 1812.

DURING THE AMERICAN REVOLUTION, THE NEW state of New York named Kingston as its capital city. The state adopted its own **constitution** in 1777. This document set up the state government. Only men were allowed to vote. They chose George Clinton as the state's first governor. The state **legislature** met for the first time on September 10, 1777.

When the war ended, the states set up a national government under the **Articles of Confederation.** This agreement gave the country a set of laws to follow. But under the Articles of Confederation,

the national government was very weak. It did not even have the power to tax. In 1787, representatives from the states got together

New York Colony before statehood

Alexander Hamilton was instrumental in getting New Yorkers to approve the new U.S. Constitution.

and drew up the U.S. Constitution.

Many New Yorkers opposed the new constitution because they thought it made the central government too powerful. Some of their concerns were answered by adding a list of personal rights to the Constitution. This list, called the Bill of Rights, grants Americans many rights, including freedom of religion and freedom of speech.

Nine states had to approve the new Constitution for it to become law. New Yorker Alexander Hamilton worked hard to get the Constitution approved. On July 26, 1788, New York became the 11th state to approve the Constitution.

The new government chose New York City as the U.S. capital. Congress met for the first time in Federal Hall in New York City on March 4, 1789. George Washington, the first president, took the oath of office there eight weeks later, on April 30. The new nation was under way. New York was at its center.

Federal Hall in New York City was the site of the first session of the U.S. Congress on March 4, 1789. It was also the location of George Washington's inauguration as first president of the United States on April 30 of that same year.

1459–1570   The Iroquois League of Five Nations is formed.

1524   Giovanni da Verrazano sails into New York Harbor.

1609   Englishman Henry Hudson, sailing for the Dutch, explores the Hudson River. Samuel de Champlain enters present-day New York from the north.

1624   Fort Orange (Albany) is established on the Hudson River.

1625   The Dutch establish the colony of New Netherland.

1629   The Dutch West India Company begins selling land in New Amsterdam (now New York City).

1664   England takes over New Netherland, renaming it New York.

1735   Newspaper publisher Peter Zenger is put on trial for printing articles attacking the English governor. This trial secures freedom of the press in the colonies.

1754   The French and Indian War begins between France and Great Britain.

1764   The British pass the Sugar Act, a tax on sugar, coffee, and cloth.

1765   The British pass the Stamp Act, a tax on all printed materials.

1767   British enact a tax on tea.

1775   Ethan Allen and the Green Mountain Boys capture Fort Ticonderoga from the British.

1776   The Declaration of Independence is signed.

1777   The Continental army defeats the British at the Battle of Saratoga.

1781   The Articles of Confederation becomes law.

1785   New York City becomes the national capital.

1788   New York becomes the eleventh state of the United States.

1789   The first Congress of the United States meets in New York City. George Washington is sworn in as the first U.S. president.

Glossary TERMS

Articles of Confederation
(AR-tik-uhls uv kon-fed-uh-RAY-shun)
The Articles of Confederation was the first constitution of the United States. It was replaced by the U.S. Constitution in 1788.

charter (CHAR-tuhr)
A charter is a document giving someone permission to set up a colony. The Dutch West India Company was given a charter to settle New Netherland in 1621.

conspiracy (kuhn-SPEE-ruh-see)
A conspiracy is a secret plot to do something wrong. In 1741, some New Yorkers feared a series of fires was a sign of a slave uprising. This became known as the New York Conspiracy.

constitution (kon-stuh-TOO-shun)
A constitution is a document setting up a government. New York state adopted its constitution in 1777.

Continental Congress
(kon-tuh-NENT-uhl KON-griss)
The Continental Congress was a meeting of colonists that served as the American government during Revolutionary times. The Second Continental Congress adopted the Declaration of Independence in 1776.

indentured servants
(in-DEN-shurd CER-vuhnts)
Indentured servants were people who agreed to work for someone else for a certain period of time in exchange for payment of travel expenses. Many of New York's first settlers were indentured servants.

league (LEEG)
A league is a union of groups with a common goal. The League of Five Nations was made up of five Iroquois groups from central New York.

legislature (LEDG-uh-slay-chuhr)
A legislature is the part of government that makes laws. The New York legislature first met in 1777.

opportunity (op-uhr-TOO-nih-tee)
An opportunity is a good chance to do something. Many people came to New York because of its economic opportunity.

representation (rep-ree-zehn-TAY-shun)
Representation is having someone else who speaks on your behalf. The American colonists claimed they were suffering "taxation without representation," because they had no representatives in the British government.

James Duane (1733–1797)

Continental Congress delegate, 1774–83; Articles of Confederation signer, 1778; U.S. senator, 1782–85, 1787–90; New York City mayor, 1784–89; U.S. district court justice for New York, 1790–94

William Duer (1747–1799)

Continental Congress delegate, 1777–79; Articles of Confederation signer; New York state legislature member, 1786

William Floyd (1734–1821)

Continental Congress delegate, 1774–77, 1778–83; Declaration of Independence signer; Congress of the Confederation delegate, 1781–1783; U.S. House of Representatives member, 1789–91

Alexander Hamilton (1755–1804)

Continental Congress delegate, 1782–83, 1787–88; New York state legislature member, 1787; Constitutional Convention member, 1787; U.S. Constitution signer; U.S. secretary of the treasury, 1789–95

John Lansing Jr. (1754–c. 1829)

Constitutional Convention delegate, 1787; New York state supreme court justice, 1790–1801

Francis Lewis (1713–1803)

Continental Congress delegate, 1774–79; Declaration of Independence signer; Articles of Confederation signer

Philip Livingston (1716–1778)

Continental Congress delegate, 1774–78; Declaration of Independence signer; U.S. senator

Gouverneur Morris (1752–1816)

Continental Congress delegate, 1778; Articles of Confederation signer; New York state assembly member, 1777–78; Constitutional Convention delegate, 1787; U.S. Minister to France, 1792–94; U.S. senator, 1800–03

Lewis Morris (1726–1798)

Continental Congress delegate, 1775–77; Declaration of Independence signer

Robert Yates (1738–1801)

New York state supreme court justice, 1777–98; Constitutional Convention delegate, 1787; New York state supreme court chief justice, 1790–98

For Further INFORMATION

Web Sites

Visit our homepage for lots of links about the New York colony:
http://www.childsworld.com/links.html

Note to Parents, Teachers, and Librarians:
We routinely verify our Web links to make sure they're safe,
active sites—so encourage your readers to check them out!

Books

Banks, Joan, and Arthur M. Schlesinger. *Peter Stuyvesant: Dutch Military Leader.* Broomall, Pa. Chelsea House, 2000.

Bruchac, Joseph. *The Arrow over the Door.* New York: Dial Books for Young Readers, 1998.

Quackenbush, Robert M. *Daughter of Liberty: A True Story of the American Revolution.* New York: Hyperion Press, 1999.

Videotapes

American Colonies/American Revolution. 2001. Directed by Bert Salzman. 66 min. Find the Fun Productions.

Places to Visit or Contact

Crown Point State Historic Site
To learn more about the history of New York during the French and Indian War and the American Revolution
739 Bridge Road
Crown Point, NY 12928
518/597-4666

Iroquois Museum
For a complete view of the lifestyle, history, and culture of the Iroquois nation
Caverns Road
Howes Cave, NY 12092
518/296-8949

Index

About the Author

Barbara Somervill is the author of many books for children. She loves learning and sees every writing project as a chance to learn new information or gain a new understanding. Ms. Somervill grew up in New York State, but has also lived in Toronto, Canada; Canberra, Australia; California; and South Carolina. She currently lives with her husband in Simpsonville, South Carolina.